National Parks

ZION NATIONAL PARK

Trudy Becker

WWW.APEXEDITIONS.COM

Copyright © 2025 by Apex Editions, Mendota Heights, MN 55120. All rights reserved. No part of this book may be reproduced or utilized in any form or by any means without written permission from the publisher.

Apex is distributed by North Star Editions:
sales@northstareditions.com | 888-417-0195

Produced for Apex by Red Line Editorial.

Photographs ©: Shutterstock Images, cover, 1, 4–5, 6–7, 8–9, 10–11, 12–13, 16–17, 18–19, 20–21, 26–27, 30–31, 32–33, 40–41, 42–43, 46–47, 50–51, 52–53, 54–55, 56–57; iStockphoto, 14–15, 29, 34–35, 36–37, 39, 48–49; US Geological Survey, 22–23; George A. Grant/National Archives, 24–25; Rebecca Alfafara/National Park Service, 44–45; Red Line Editorial, 58; National Park Service, 58–59

Library of Congress Control Number: 2024943627

ISBN
979-8-89250-458-4 (hardcover)
979-8-89250-474-4 (paperback)
979-8-89250-505-5 (ebook pdf)
979-8-89250-490-4 (hosted ebook)

Printed in the United States of America
Mankato, MN
012025

NOTE TO PARENTS AND EDUCATORS

Apex books are designed to build literacy skills in striving readers. Exciting, high-interest content attracts and holds readers' attention. The text is carefully leveled to allow students to achieve success quickly.

TABLE OF CONTENTS

Chapter 1
THROUGH THE CANYON 4

Chapter 2
ALL ABOUT ZION 9

Chapter 3
PEOPLE AND ZION 18

Natural Wonder
CHECKERBOARD MESA 28

Chapter 4
FUN AT ZION 31

Natural Wonder
THE NARROWS 38

Chapter 5
WILDLIFE 40

Chapter 6
SAVING ZION 50

PARK MAP • 58
COMPREHENSION QUESTIONS • 60
GLOSSARY • 62
TO LEARN MORE • 63
ABOUT THE AUTHOR • 63
INDEX • 64

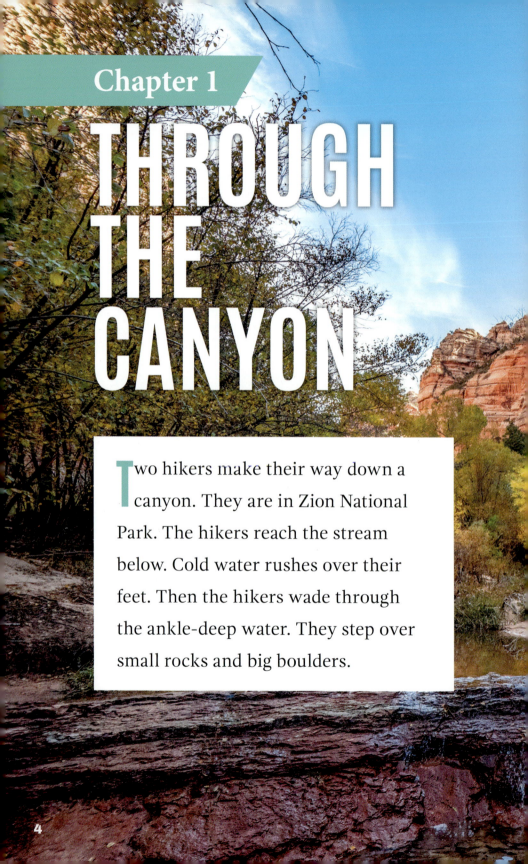

Chapter 1

THROUGH THE CANYON

Two hikers make their way down a canyon. They are in Zion National Park. The hikers reach the stream below. Cold water rushes over their feet. Then the hikers wade through the ankle-deep water. They step over small rocks and big boulders.

Canyons are found mostly in dry places with little rain.

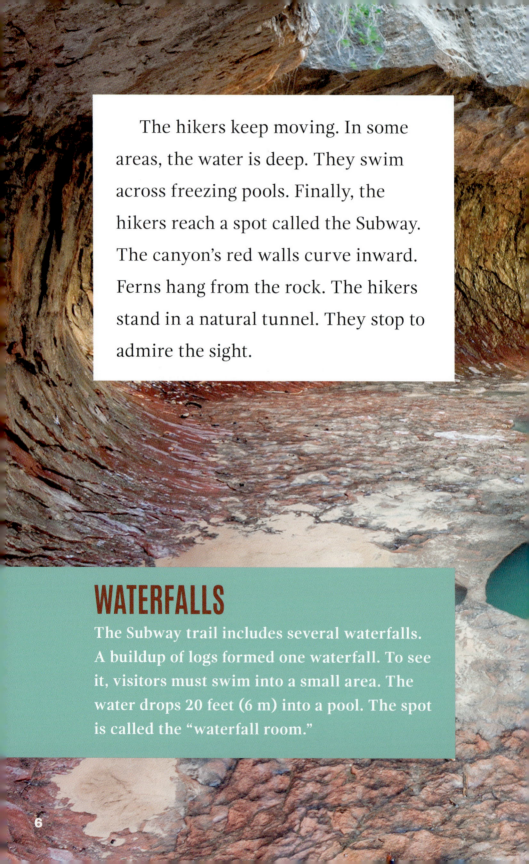

The hikers keep moving. In some areas, the water is deep. They swim across freezing pools. Finally, the hikers reach a spot called the Subway. The canyon's red walls curve inward. Ferns hang from the rock. The hikers stand in a natural tunnel. They stop to admire the sight.

WATERFALLS

The Subway trail includes several waterfalls. A buildup of logs formed one waterfall. To see it, visitors must swim into a small area. The water drops 20 feet (6 m) into a pool. The spot is called the "waterfall room."

The Subway trail is for hikers with lots of experience.

Zion is one of five national parks in the state of Utah.

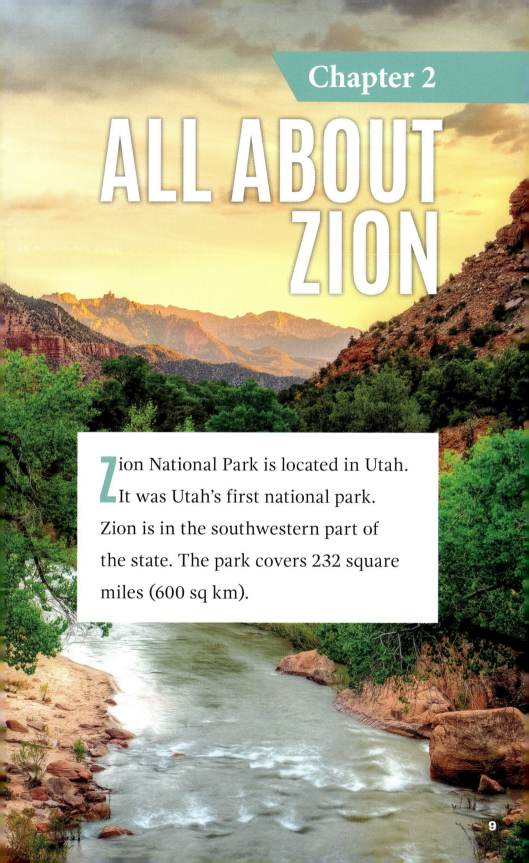

Chapter 2
ALL ABOUT ZION

Zion National Park is located in Utah. It was Utah's first national park. Zion is in the southwestern part of the state. The park covers 232 square miles (600 sq km).

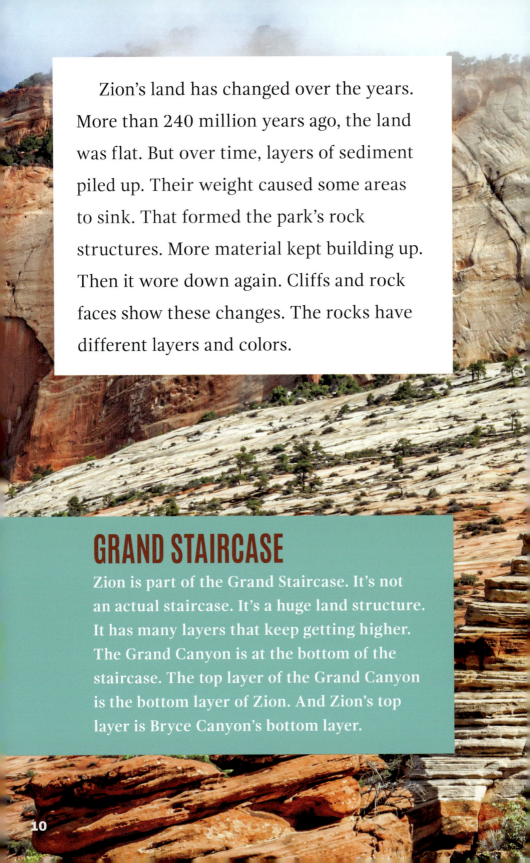

Zion's land has changed over the years. More than 240 million years ago, the land was flat. But over time, layers of sediment piled up. Their weight caused some areas to sink. That formed the park's rock structures. More material kept building up. Then it wore down again. Cliffs and rock faces show these changes. The rocks have different layers and colors.

GRAND STAIRCASE

Zion is part of the Grand Staircase. It's not an actual staircase. It's a huge land structure. It has many layers that keep getting higher. The Grand Canyon is at the bottom of the staircase. The top layer of the Grand Canyon is the bottom layer of Zion. And Zion's top layer is Bryce Canyon's bottom layer.

Rocks with many layers are called sedimentary rocks.

Water carved the park's shape, too. The Virgin River runs through Zion. Over time, the river cut through the rock. This formed Zion's main canyon. The river still carves the land today. It carries tons of sediment. It also carries rocks and fallen trees. These objects slowly wear down the stone.

NATURAL TEMPLE

The Temple of Sinawava is near the Virgin River. The structure has curved rock walls. It looks like a theater. There is even a central rock formation. The spot looks like a podium for speakers.

The Pa'rus Trail goes along part of the Virgin River.

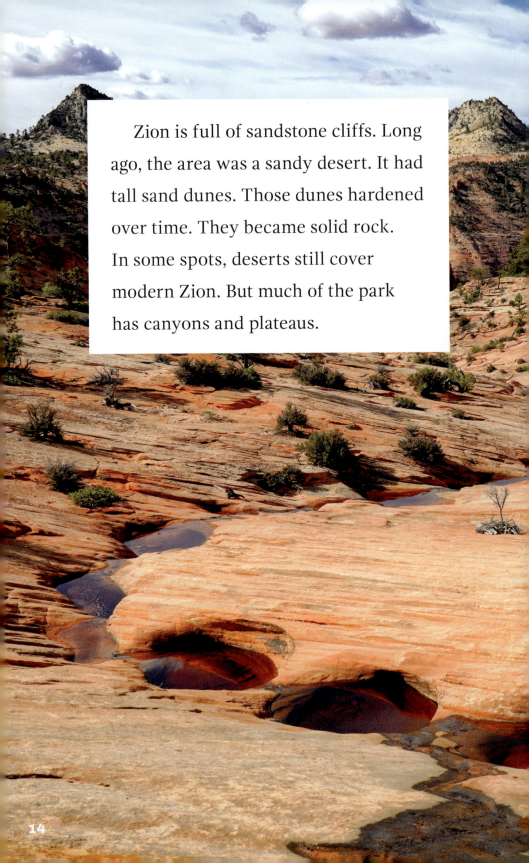

Zion is full of sandstone cliffs. Long ago, the area was a sandy desert. It had tall sand dunes. Those dunes hardened over time. They became solid rock. In some spots, deserts still cover modern Zion. But much of the park has canyons and plateaus.

The color of sandstone depends on the amount of iron in the rock.

Most of Zion is rock. But the park includes other types of land, too. Some of the area is forested. Many trees are evergreens, such as fir trees. Zion also has some wetlands. These are close to the park's main rivers and streams.

PAST FORESTS
Fossils in Zion offer glimpses of the past. Some fossils show part of old trees. These trees died millions of years ago. The fossils help scientists learn how the area used to be.

More than 1,000 kinds of plants grow at Zion National Park.

PEOPLE AND ZION

People have lived near Zion for thousands of years. Early humans hunted big animals there. Over time, many Indigenous peoples made their homes in Zion. For example, Ancestral Puebloan and Fremont peoples lived in the area.

Ancient people carved artwork into the rocks at Zion.

By 1000 CE, the people near Zion were mostly Southern Paiutes. The desert land wasn't easy to farm. But the river helped. The Southern Paiutes used its water. They grew a variety of crops. These included corn, melons, and pumpkins. Southern Paiutes also hunted large animals such as elk and deer.

LIFE IN ZION

Ancient Indigenous peoples created stone tools. They also wove baskets and blankets. Modern Zion still shows evidence of their settlements. People have found pieces of old cliff houses. They found rock art, too.

Mule deer are common at Zion.

In the late 1700s, white fur-trappers arrived in the area. And in the 1800s, government surveyors came. White settlers began making homes in the area, too. The settlers took over Indigenous people's land. They also enslaved Indigenous people.

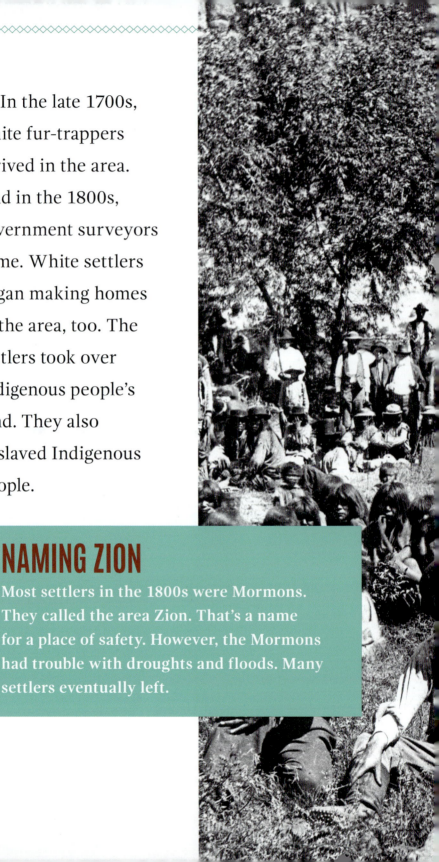

NAMING ZION

Most settlers in the 1800s were Mormons. They called the area Zion. That's a name for a place of safety. However, the Mormons had trouble with droughts and floods. Many settlers eventually left.

Government surveyors meet with Southern Paiutes in the 1870s.

A group of visitors pose for a picture in the 1920s.

In the early 1900s, more surveyors came to Zion. So did artists. Word spread about the area's beauty. Soon, people started a campaign. They asked the US government to set aside the land. That way, it could be protected. In 1919, Zion became a national park.

PAIUTE PEOPLE TODAY

In the 1950s, the US government made a decision. It said the Southern Paiutes were no longer a nation. However, the government changed this decision in 1980. Many Southern Paiute people still live near the park today. They help protect the land.

REACHING THE SIGHTS

In the early 1900s, tourism began in the area. More people came to see the rock structures. However, the roads were bad. There was no railroad nearby, either. For a while, it was difficult for visitors to reach the area. That began to change in the 1920s.

The Zion-Mount Carmel Tunnel and highway took nearly three years to build.

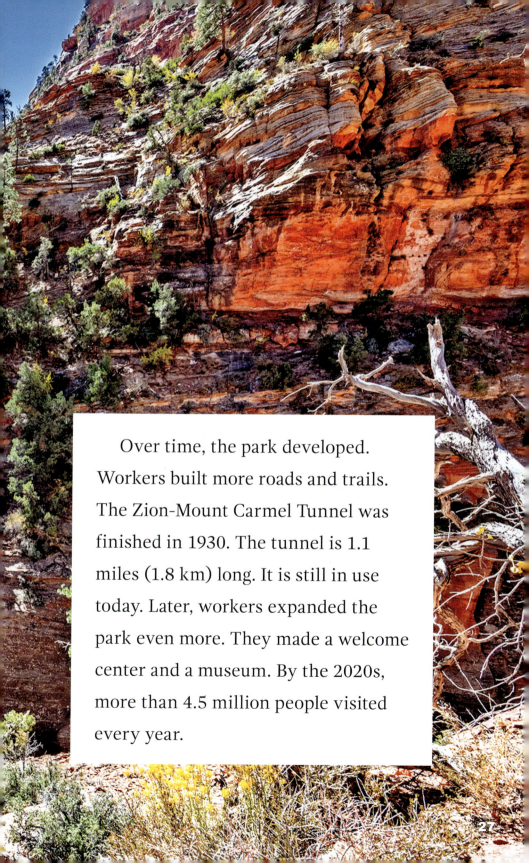

Over time, the park developed. Workers built more roads and trails. The Zion-Mount Carmel Tunnel was finished in 1930. The tunnel is 1.1 miles (1.8 km) long. It is still in use today. Later, workers expanded the park even more. They made a welcome center and a museum. By the 2020s, more than 4.5 million people visited every year.

Natural Wonder
CHECKERBOARD MESA

Checkerboard Mesa is one of Zion's most iconic landmarks. The mesa is a big sandstone hill. It towers 900 feet (275 m). Visitors can view the structure from the road. Or they can hike up it.

The mesa has a cracked pattern. It looks like the squares of a checkerboard. The structure's pattern formed over millions of years. Vertical lines came from the rock baking in sunny daylight. Then it cooled at night. Horizontal lines came from erosion. Wind wore away layers over time.

Checkerboard Mesa is surrounded by pine forest.

Camping can be very hot in Zion. Sometimes, there is no shade.

Chapter 4
FUN AT ZION

Zion offers activities for all kinds of visitors. Some people arrive for a day trip. They just want to see the main sights. Others stay for longer visits. Many people camp in the park. Zion has three main campgrounds. The park also has areas for overnight backpacking.

Hiking is a main attraction at Zion. The park has 90 miles (145 km) of trails. The trails cover different types of landscape. Some trails are great for beginners. Pa'rus Trail is one example. The path is open to wheelchairs, bikes, and pets. Other trails are very difficult. Angels Landing is the most famous.

KOLOB ARCH

Kolob Arch is a natural arch. It is one of the biggest in the world. The arch spans 287 feet (87 m). Visitors can hike to the arch. But it's not easy. The arch is 7 miles (11 km) from the nearest road.

Angels Landing is very steep. Hikers hold on to chains as they climb up.

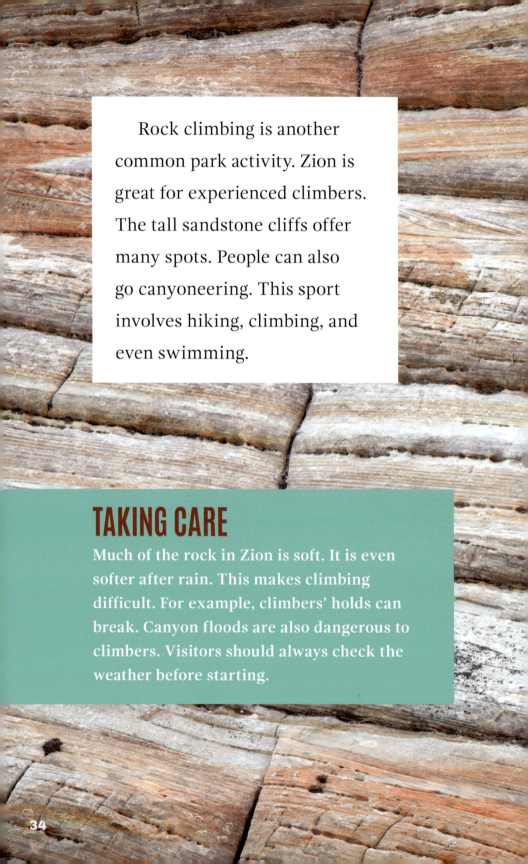

Rock climbing is another common park activity. Zion is great for experienced climbers. The tall sandstone cliffs offer many spots. People can also go canyoneering. This sport involves hiking, climbing, and even swimming.

TAKING CARE

Much of the rock in Zion is soft. It is even softer after rain. This makes climbing difficult. For example, climbers' holds can break. Canyon floods are also dangerous to climbers. Visitors should always check the weather before starting.

Rock climbers use maps to plan their routes.

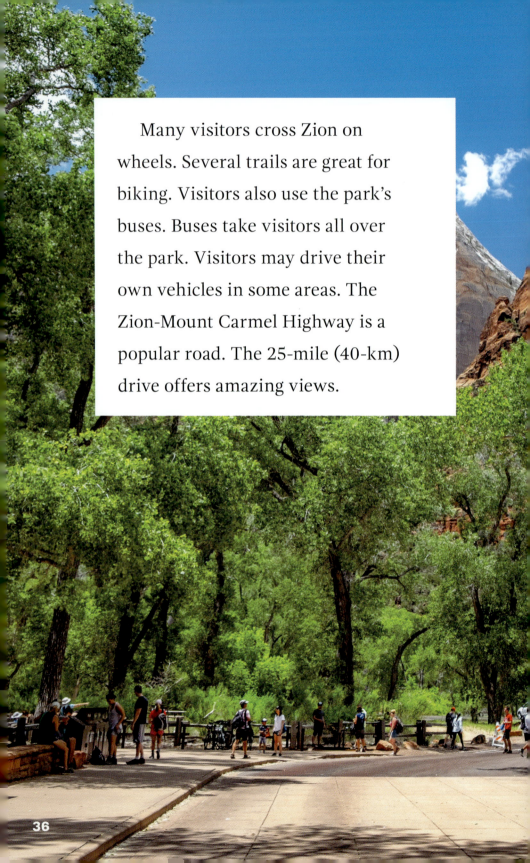

Many visitors cross Zion on wheels. Several trails are great for biking. Visitors also use the park's buses. Buses take visitors all over the park. Visitors may drive their own vehicles in some areas. The Zion-Mount Carmel Highway is a popular road. The 25-mile (40-km) drive offers amazing views.

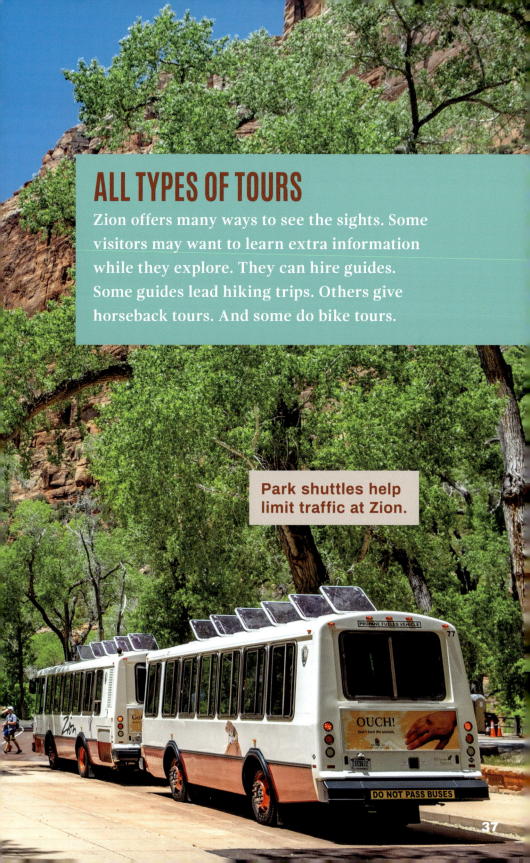

ALL TYPES OF TOURS

Zion offers many ways to see the sights. Some visitors may want to learn extra information while they explore. They can hire guides. Some guides lead hiking trips. Others give horseback tours. And some do bike tours.

Park shuttles help limit traffic at Zion.

Natural Wonder
THE NARROWS

The Narrows is an iconic Zion attraction. The Narrows is the narrowest part of Zion Canyon. People can hike this section of the river.

The Virgin River runs along the canyon's bottom. The Narrows takes hikers straight through the water. So, people must be ready to get wet. Some areas are shallow. Water reaches hikers' ankles. In other spots, water is deep. Water can be chest-high or deeper. Hikers may even have to swim.

> **Many visitors use hiking poles to keep their balance in the Narrows.**

Chapter 5

WILDLIFE

Zion is best known for its landscapes. But the park is full of wildlife, too. Different habitats support many kinds of wildlife. Some live in the desert areas. Others make homes in canyons and trees. Zion has river wildlife, too.

Bobcats live in Zion National Park, but they are a rare sight.

More than 70 kinds of mammals live in Zion. Rock squirrels are one common type. So are bighorn sheep. They climb along rocky surfaces. Mule deer can be seen in the area, too. These deer have large ears, which help them stay cool in the desert. Mountain lions and porcupines also make their homes in Zion.

RINGTAILS

Ringtails are members of the raccoon family. They only come out at night. Most visitors never see them. But ringtails climb all around the park. Tiny claws help them scale rocks, cliffs, and trees. They hunt insects and other small mammals.

Rock squirrels can go more than three months without water.

43

Birds are a key part of Zion's wildlife. For example, condors live in the park. So do falcons. These birds lay eggs on cliff ledges. Great roadrunners live in the desert. These birds can run 15 miles per hour (24 km/h).

OWLS

Nine types of owl live in Zion. The Mexican spotted owl is threatened. Its population is decreasing. But Zion has 15 nesting sites of these owls. They stay in Zion's cooler canyons.

California condors are endangered. Scientists track them using numbered tags.

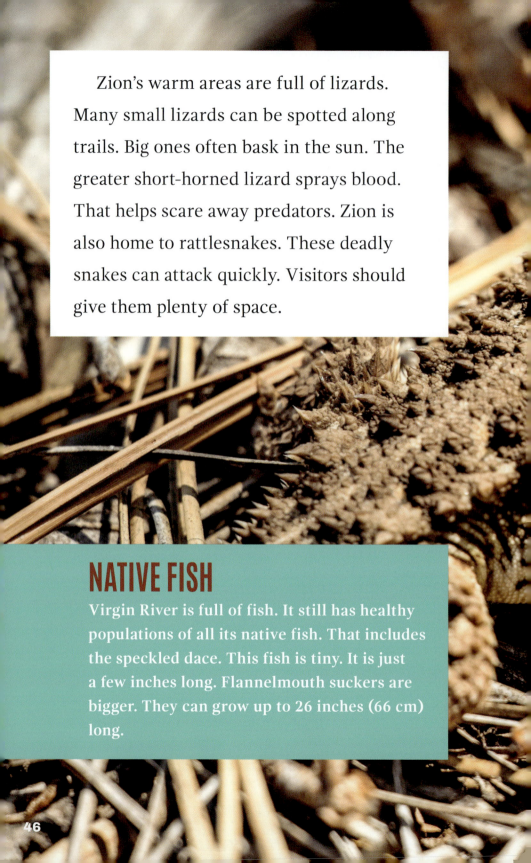

Zion's warm areas are full of lizards. Many small lizards can be spotted along trails. Big ones often bask in the sun. The greater short-horned lizard sprays blood. That helps scare away predators. Zion is also home to rattlesnakes. These deadly snakes can attack quickly. Visitors should give them plenty of space.

NATIVE FISH

Virgin River is full of fish. It still has healthy populations of all its native fish. That includes the speckled dace. This fish is tiny. It is just a few inches long. Flannelmouth suckers are bigger. They can grow up to 26 inches (66 cm) long.

Short-horned lizards have sharp bumps that stop predators from eating them.

47

Plants are key to Zion's biodiversity. More than 1,000 species of plants are found in the park. In the deserts, prickly pears are common. So are yuccas. These plants can survive with little water. Cottonwood trees do well near the river. Higher areas have fir and pine trees.

Yucca plants can be made into rope and other materials.

Chapter 6

SAVING ZION

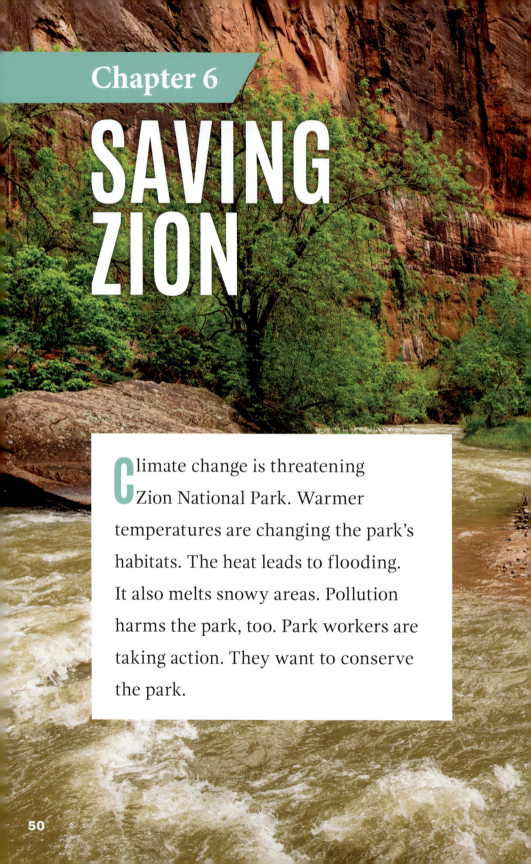

Climate change is threatening Zion National Park. Warmer temperatures are changing the park's habitats. The heat leads to flooding. It also melts snowy areas. Pollution harms the park, too. Park workers are taking action. They want to conserve the park.

Flash floods can happen at any time. They can be dangerous to hikers.

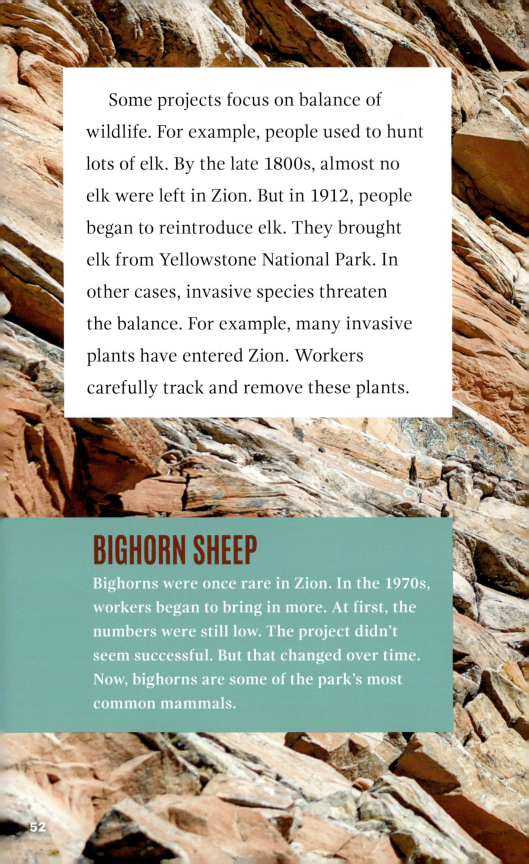

Some projects focus on balance of wildlife. For example, people used to hunt lots of elk. By the late 1800s, almost no elk were left in Zion. But in 1912, people began to reintroduce elk. They brought elk from Yellowstone National Park. In other cases, invasive species threaten the balance. For example, many invasive plants have entered Zion. Workers carefully track and remove these plants.

BIGHORN SHEEP

Bighorns were once rare in Zion. In the 1970s, workers began to bring in more. At first, the numbers were still low. The project didn't seem successful. But that changed over time. Now, bighorns are some of the park's most common mammals.

Bighorn sheep are excellent climbers.

Many park projects focus on saving habitats. Rising heat has led to big changes in some rivers and streams. For example, dangerous bacteria grow better in warmer water. This harms park wildlife. It can harm people, too. So, park workers test the water quality often. They check levels of bacteria, pesticides, and more.

NEARBY LAND

Zion workers want to protect the entire environment. That includes the land near the park. So, park workers teamed up with others. They made plans with people on private land nearby. These people agreed to help take care of the habitat.

Bacteria can cause illness if people drink from Zion's rivers and streams.

Many visitors come to Zion. That can harm the environment, too. But the park has made big changes. For example, fewer cars are allowed in the park. This cuts down on pollution. The park also updated its buses. They use less fuel. Newer buildings use less energy, too. And they make less waste. All these actions help the land and wildlife. That way, visitors can keep enjoying Zion in the future.

Visitors can help keep the park clean by not littering.

PARK MAP

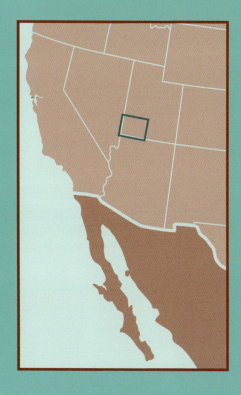

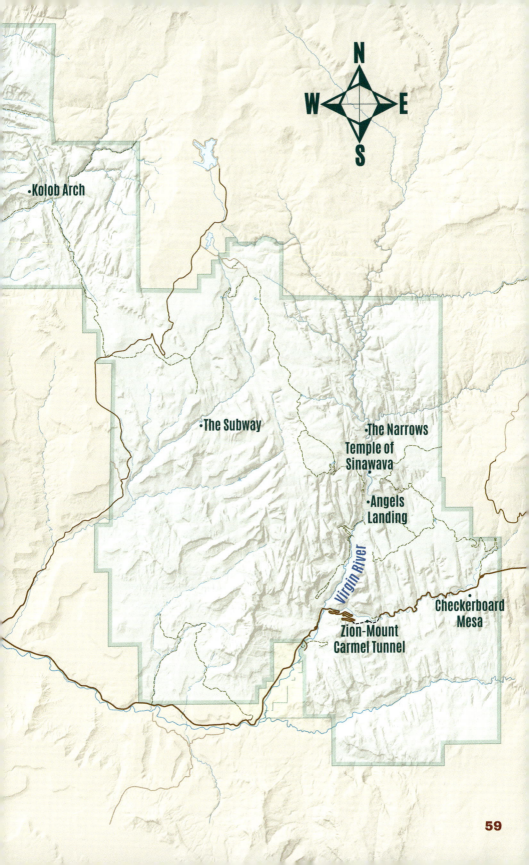

COMPREHENSION QUESTIONS

Write your answers on a separate piece of paper.

1. Write a few sentences describing types of animals that live in Zion National Park.

2. Do you think people are doing enough to conserve the park? Why or why not?

3. Where did the park's sandstone cliffs come from?

    A. old sand dunes
    B. old forests
    C. old campgrounds

4. Why do people want to keep invasive plants out of Zion?

    A. Park workers do not like how the plants look.
    B. Invasive plants could harm native wildlife.
    C. The habitat is too empty for new plants.

5. What does **campaign** mean in this book?

*Word spread about the area's beauty. Soon, people started a **campaign**. They asked the US government to set aside the land.*

    A. a set of actions that are meant to convince people of something
    B. a set of actions that are meant to make a place more beautiful
    C. a set of actions that are meant to make people dislike something

6. What does **biodiversity** mean in this book?

*Plants are key to Zion's **biodiversity**. More than 1,000 species of plants are found in the park.*

    A. when a place has one kind of living thing
    B. when a place has no living things
    C. when a place has many kinds of living things

Answer key on page 32.

GLOSSARY

canyon
A deep cut in the ground that has steep sides.

climate change
A dangerous long-term change in Earth's temperature and weather patterns.

fossils
Remains of plants and animals that lived long ago.

Indigenous
Related to the original people who lived in an area.

invasive
Spreading quickly in a new area and causing many problems there.

mammals
Animals that have hair and produce milk for their young.

native
Originally living in an area.

pollution
Things that are dirty or unsafe.

sediment
Tiny pieces of solid material moved by water or wind.

species
Groups of animals or plants that are similar and can breed with one another.

surveyors
People who study land to make maps.

TO LEARN MORE

BOOKS

Bowman, Chris. *Zion National Park*. Minneapolis: Bellwether Media, 2023.

Drimmer, Stephanie Warren. *Ultimate Mammalpedia*. Washington, DC: National Geographic Kids, 2023.

London, Martha. *Utah*. Minneapolis: Abdo Publishing, 2023.

ONLINE RESOURCES

Visit **www.apexeditions.com** to find links and resources related to this title.

ABOUT THE AUTHOR

Trudy Becker lives in Minneapolis, Minnesota. She likes exploring new places and loves anything involving books.

INDEX

Angels Landing, 32

bighorn sheep, 42, 52
biking, 32, 36–37
birds, 44

camping, 31
canyoneering, 34
Checkerboard Mesa, 28
climate change, 50
conservation, 50, 52, 54–56

elk, 20, 52

forests, 16
fossils, 16

Grand Staircase, 10

hiking, 4, 6, 28, 32, 34, 37, 38

Indigenous peoples, 18, 20, 22
invasive species, 52

Kolob Arch, 32

lizards, 46

Narrows, the, 38

Pa'rus Trail, 32
plants, 48, 52

ringtails, 42
rock climbing, 34

snakes, 46
Southern Paiute people, 20, 25
Subway Trail, 6
swimming, 6, 34, 38

Temple of Sinawava, 13
trails, 6, 27, 32, 36, 46

Virgin River, 12–13, 38, 46

waterfalls, 6

Zion-Mount Carmel Tunnel, 27

ANSWER KEY:
1. Answers will vary; 2. Answers will vary; 3. A; 4. B; 5. A; 6. C